THE WONDERS OF OUR WORLD

Hurricanes
& Tornadoes

Neil Morris

CRABTREE PUBLISHING COMPANY

www.crabtreebooks.com

The Wonders of our World

Crabtree Publishing Company

PMB 16A
350 Fifth Avenue
Suite 3308
New York, N.Y. 10118

612 Welland Avenue
St. Catharines
Ontario, Canada
L2M 5V6

73 Lime Walk
Headington
Oxford OX3 7AD
United Kingdom

Author: Neil Morris
Managing editor: Jackie Fortey
Editors: Penny Clarke and Greg Nickles
Designer: Richard Rowan
Art director: Chris Legee
Picture research: Robert Francis

Picture Credits:
Artists: David Ashby 8, 27 (bottom); Peter Bull Studio 14, 15, 26, 27 (top);
John Hutchison 6, 18; Paul Williams 4
Maps: AND Map Graphics Ltd. 7, 12, 15, 17, 24
Photographs: Abbie Enock 18; Robert Francis 3, 6, 10, 11 (bottom), 22,
23 (top), 26, 28-29; Ronald Grant Archive 16; Robert Harding Picture Library
cover, title page, 16-17, 19 (top), 21 (bottom); Hutchison Library 9 (top),
10-11; Panos Pictures 7, 11 (top), 12-13, 13, 23 (bottom), 25 (top), 29 (bottom);
Pictor International 5 (bottom), 14, 15; Science Photo Library 5 (top), 8-9,
9 (bottom), 20, 20-21, 21, 24; Stock Market Photo Agency 28; Topham Picture
Point 17, 19 (bottom); Weather Channel, USA 29 (top); ZEFA 25 (bottom).
All other photographs by Digital Stock and Digital Vision.

Cataloging-in-publication data

Morris, Neil
          Hurricanes and tornadoes / Neil Morris
p. cm. — (The wonders of our world)
Includes index.
ISBN 0-86505-831-8 (library bound) ISBN 0-86505-843-1 (pbk.)
Summary: Introduces the different types of hurricanes and
tornadoes, their histories, and effects on humans.
1. Hurricanes—Juvenile literature. 2. Tornadoes—Juvenile
literature. [1. Hurricanes. 2. Tornadoes.] I. Title. II. Series:
Morris, Neil. Wonders of our world.

QC944.2.M67 1998   j551.55'2   LC 98-11203 CIP

CONTENTS

WHAT IS A HURRICANE?

A HURRICANE is a large, powerful storm with very high winds. It starts over the ocean, and often causes great damage when it moves over land. Its winds can blow at speeds of over 75 miles (120 kilometers) per hour, and the whole whirling storm travels at about 12 miles (20 kilometers) per hour. At sea, hurricanes bring heavy rain and high waves, which often cause floods along coasts.

INSIDE THE SPINNING STORM

The illustration below is cutaway to show clouds and winds spinning around a calm area, called the eye, in the center of a hurricane. The eye may be 9 to 19 miles (15 to 30 kilometers) across. Thick, whirling clouds form a wall around the eye, and these are surrounded by more bands of rain clouds. Air is sucked towards the center of the storm and then moves upwards at great speed. The whole hurricane may measure over 250 miles (400 kilometers) across.

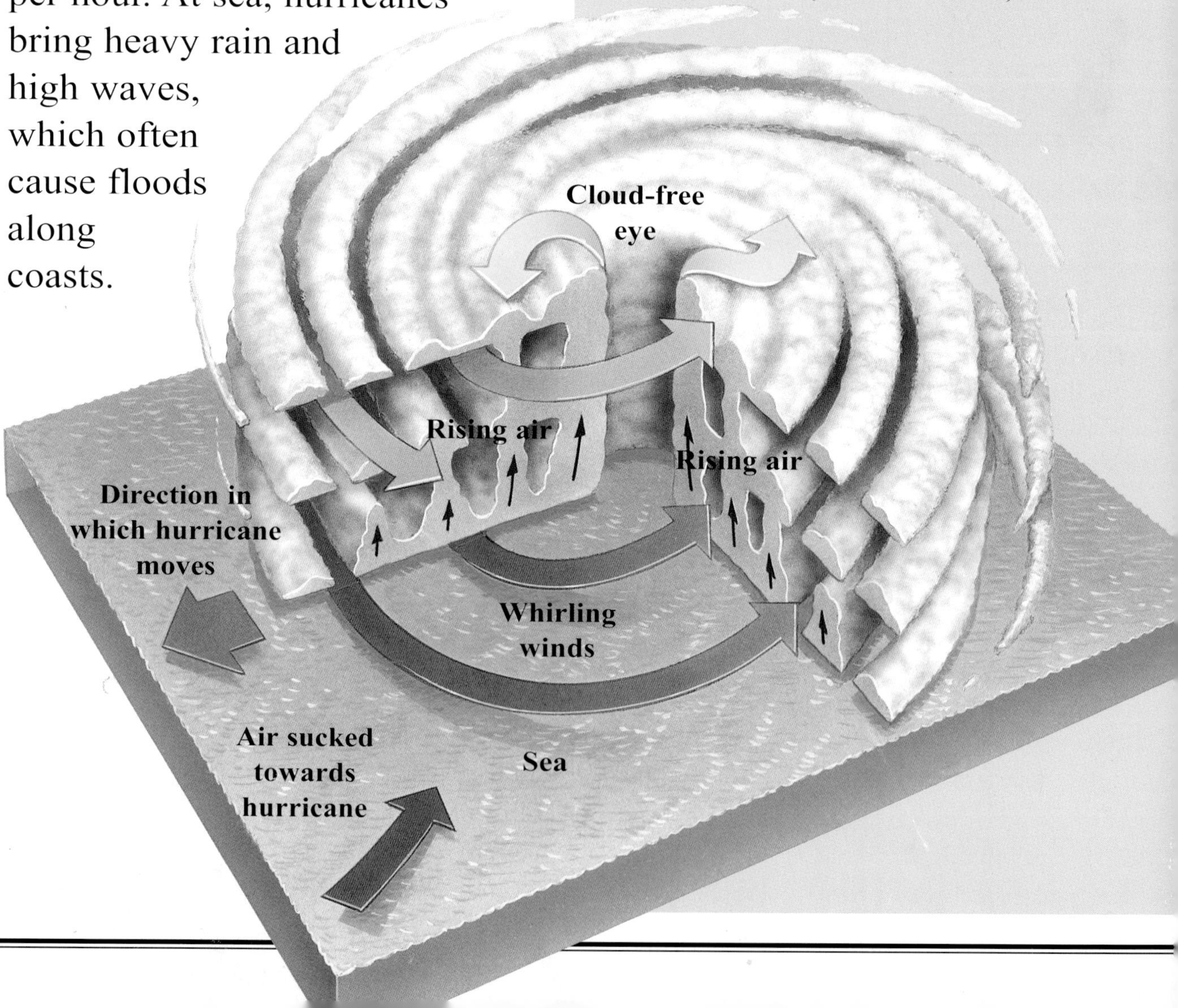

Cloud-free eye

Rising air

Rising air

Direction in which hurricane moves

Whirling winds

Air sucked towards hurricane

Sea

SEEN FROM SPACE

This hurricane's eye is easy to see in the photograph above, taken from a space shuttle. North of the equator, a hurricane's winds blow around the eye in a counter-clockwise direction. South of the equator, hurricane winds blow clockwise.

COMING ASHORE

HURRICANE winds batter trees and houses in the Caribbean (below).

The first winds and rain are followed by calm for up to an hour as the eye of the storm passes. Then more rain and strong winds come.

THE WORLD'S HURRICANES

HURRICANES START over warm ocean waters in regions near the equator, called the tropics. In these regions, the high sea temperatures can cause warm, moist air to rise. As the air rises, it turns in an upward spiral. More air rushes in underneath the rising air. Then it too rises and spins, building up to form a hurricane. In the western Pacific Ocean, these storms are called typhoons, from the Chinese word for "great winds." In the Indian Ocean, they are known as cyclones.

STORM SURGE

Tropical storms whip up the water of the warm oceans (right). In addition, the eye of the storm pulls a mound of water up to 26 feet (8 meters) high. The waves produce a storm surge, which can cause flooding when it reaches land.

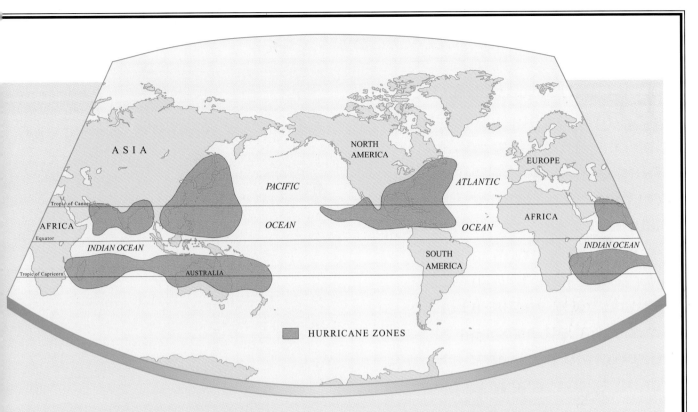

ASIA		NORTH AMERICA		EUROPE	
	PACIFIC		ATLANTIC		
Tropic of Cancer		OCEAN		AFRICA	
AFRICA	OCEAN				
Equator					
INDIAN OCEAN			SOUTH	INDIAN OCEAN	
Tropic of Capricorn	AUSTRALIA		AMERICA		

☐ HURRICANE ZONES

TROPICAL STORM CLOUDS

Storm clouds gather over the South China Sea (left). This part of the western Pacific Ocean lies between the equator and the tropic of Cancer. In summer, its waters may reach 84° Fahrenheit (29° Celsius), helping cause many typhoons.

WHERE IN THE WORLD?

Scientists, called meteorologists, who study weather often refer to hurricanes and typhoons as tropical cyclones. The world map above shows where they most often occur. They usually start in a band just north and south of the equator.

CYCLONE FLOODS

THIS flood in Bangladesh (right), in Asia, was caused by a cyclone. As the winds and rains raced in from the Indian Ocean, a storm surge flooded the low-lying land of the Ganges delta.

ATLANTIC HURRICANES

DURING MOST years, six to eight hurricanes develop in the Atlantic Ocean. Each one lasts about six days. They occur mainly between July and October, when the ocean's waters are warm. Once formed, hurricanes are blown westward by the trade winds. Many pass through the Caribbean Sea and the Gulf of Mexico, turning north before reaching land. Hurricanes gradually die out over the land, which is cooler.

ATLANTIC STORMS

ONLY a few of the many thunderstorms that occur over the Atlantic Ocean turn into hurricanes. Hurricanes have always been a big problem for shipping, especially in the days of wooden sailing ships. These old vessels were easily blown off course by the hurricanes' raging winds.

HURRICANE FRAN

Hurricane Fran, shown above, was photographed from a satellite as it neared the coast of Florida, USA, in September 1996. It then turned north toward Louisiana. Each year, meteorologists give hurricanes alternate female and male names, starting at "A." Hurricane Fran was the sixth hurricane of 1996.

DAMAGE AND DESTRUCTION

SOME of the damage caused by Hurricane Alan, in Dominica in 1980, is shown above. Vehicles were crushed and wooden houses smashed to matchwood by the raging winds and heavy rains. Everything inside the houses was flung far and wide by the wind.

THE EYE

The top of the eye of this hurricane (right) is shown from space. Every cyclone builds around an area of very low air pressure, which becomes the eye. Like a top, the winds spin around the cloud-free eye. The air within the eye is so calm that birds trapped inside can stay in the air and ride with the storm.

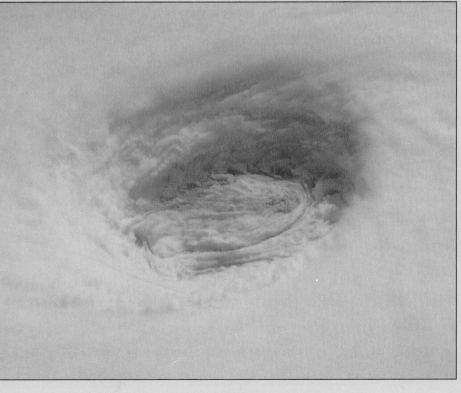

PACIFIC TYPHOONS

EACH YEAR, up to 25 typhoons occur in the northern Pacific Ocean, which is above the equator. They happen between the months of June and November. Like Atlantic hurricanes, typhoons travel westward. Many pass through the South China Sea.

In the southern Pacific, below the equator, cyclones, or "willy-willies" as the Australians call them, are most common between December and March.

FIJIAN ISLAND
The islands of Fiji lie in the Pacific south-west. Their rainy season, from November to April, sometimes brings typhoons, which cause great damage to the houses (below).

STORM APPROACHING

The dark clouds of the typhoon above are approaching the Philippines, an island country in the northwestern Pacific. In some years, more than a hundred typhoons cross the Philippines on their way to the South China Sea.

RAINY SEASON

The man above heads for shelter in Manila, the capital of the Philippines. The region's rainy season lasts from June to February. Manila's 6.7 million inhabitants are used to the rain, but fear the ferocious typhoons.

SHELTERED HARBOR

HONG Kong is one of the busiest ports in the world. It lies on the Chinese coast, on the South China Sea, a region often hit by typhoons. Some of its harbors form shelters from the typhoons, protecting boats from the high winds and waves.

INDIAN CYCLONES

THERE ARE up to 15 cyclones each year in the Indian Ocean. About half of them start north of the equator and head northward, striking lands to the west or east of India. Most of these cyclones occur at the end of the monsoon season in October.

Cyclones that start to the south of the equator usually happen in December and head southward, toward the large island of Madagascar.

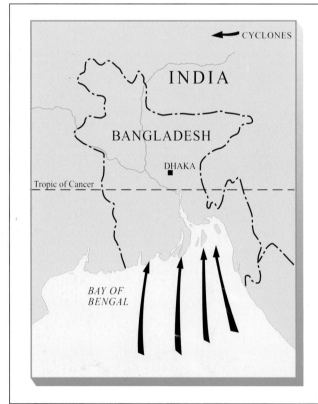

BAY OF BENGAL

IN Bangladesh, to the northeast of India, the Ganges River pours into the Bay of Bengal. This flat land is easily flooded. Monsoon winds blow from the Indian Ocean from mid-May to October. Cyclones come toward the end of this season, often causing disastrous floods.

HOMELESS

In Bangladesh (above), the monsoon rains often cause floods because the many channels of the Ganges delta overflow. Cyclones and their storm surges, coming from the Bay of Bengal, make the flooding worse. A cyclone in 1991 caused floods in which up to 10 million people in Bangladesh lost their homes.

EMERGENCY AID

Bangladeshis flooded out of their homes stand in line to receive food at an emergency center (below). Bangladesh is one of the world's most densely populated countries. Many of the 120 million Bangladeshis are farmers struggling to grow rice, fruit, and other crops on very small plots of land. When cyclones strike the region and flood the land, the people often are in desperate need of emergency food and shelter.

WHAT IS A TORNADO?

A TORNADO is a whirlwind that hangs down from a dark thundercloud and touches the ground. Tornadoes are much smaller than hurricanes, but their winds are stronger. Tornadoes form along an area called a front, where warm, moist air meets cold, dry air. The warm air rises, and as more warm air rushes in to replace it, it starts to spin and form a tornado. As with hurricanes, the winds of a tornado whirl counterclockwise in the northern hemisphere.

SPINNING FUNNEL

The funnel of a very small tornado may be only 10 feet (3 meters) wide. A big tornado might be a hundred times wider. A tornado's winds whirl at more than 200 miles (320 kilometers) per hour.

INSIDE A TORNADO

THIS diagram (left) shows warm, moist air spinning upward at tremendous speed. It creates a tornado, which is pushed along with the thundercloud by winds higher up in the sky. The diagram to the right shows how several small tornadoes may form inside a large one.

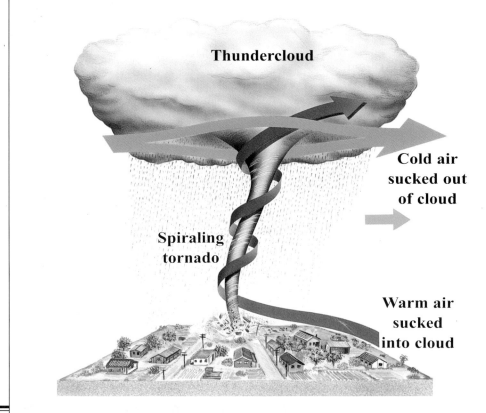

Thundercloud

Cold air sucked out of cloud

Spiraling tornado

Warm air sucked into cloud

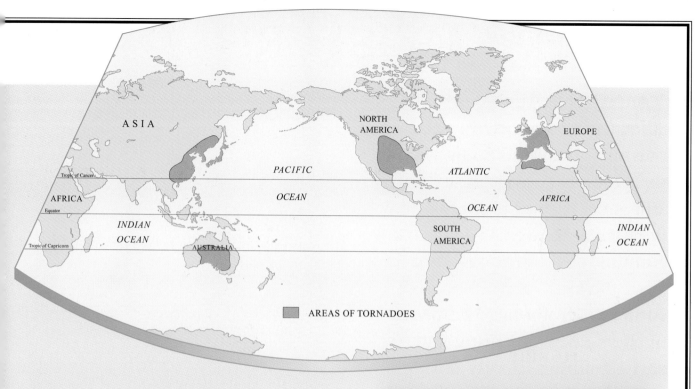

AREAS OF TORNADOES

WHERE IN THE WORLD?

Tornadoes occur all over the world, but they are most common in North America, Europe, east Asia, and Australia.

PATH OF DESTRUCTION

Most tornadoes move across the ground at 22 to 40 miles (35 to 65 kilometers) an hour. This photo of a town in Kentucky, USA (above), shows roofs lifted off and windows and doors blown out by a tornado.

TWISTER!

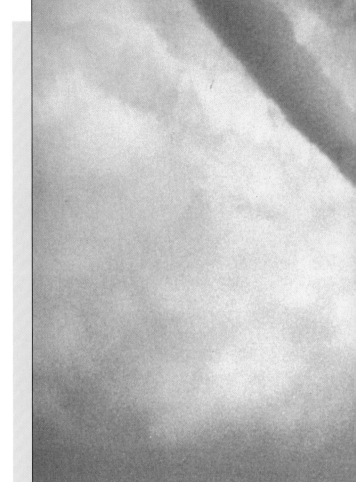

I**N NORTH** America, tornadoes are often called twisters. About 700 twisters are reported every year in the USA, and smaller ones probably take the total up to 1,000. They form along a front between warm air from the Gulf of Mexico and cooler air from the north. Most twisters occur in spring and early summer, usually during the afternoon or early evening.

Some twisters last for just ten minutes and travel only a short distance. Only one in every 200 travels more than 100 miles (160 kilometers).

Don't breathe. Don't look back.

TWISTER

The Dark Side of Nature.

UNIVERSAL PICTURES and WARNER BROS. Present An AMBLIN ENTERTAINMENT Production
HELEN HUNT BILL PAXTON "TWISTER" JAMI GERTZ and CARY ELWES Editor MICHAEL KAHN, A.C.E. Production Designer JOSEPH NEMEC III Director of Photography
Music MARK MANCINA Executive Producers STEVEN SPIELBERG, WALTER PARKES, LAURIE MacDONALD and GERALD R. MOLEN Written by MICHAEL CRICHTON & A...
Read The Arrow [Paperback] INTERNET ADDRESS http://www.uip.com Produced by KATHLEEN KENNEDY, IAN BRYCE and MICHAEL CRICHTON Directed by JAN D...

DISASTER MOVIE

H**OLLYWOOD** movies such as this one (left) use amazing special effects to simulate tornadoes. Some home moviemakers always keep a video camera nearby so that they can capture a real tornado whenever it strikes.

TERRIBLE WINDS

ON March 1, 1997, a terrible twister ripped into the state of Arkansas, USA (right). Twenty-four people died and 1,400 were left homeless by winds of up to 260 miles (420 kilometers) per hour. A previous killer twister had struck the state just one year earlier.

VIOLENT WEATHER

This tall twister (left) was photographed in Nebraska, USA, more than 750 miles (1 200 kilometers) north of the Gulf of Mexico. As a funnel cloud such as this one extends down to earth, it makes a hissing sound. When it hits the ground, the hiss turns into a loud roar.

TORNADO ALLEY

Texas and the southern US states that surround it, leading up to the Great Plains, are sometimes called "tornado alley" (below). Texas records more twisters than any other state.

WATERSPOUTS

A WATERSPOUT is a tornado that forms over water. These storms are usually much less violent than land tornadoes, with wind speeds of less than 50 miles (80 kilometers) per hour.

Even though they are not as powerful as tornadoes, waterspouts can cause great damage to ships and boats. They are common in the South China Sea, as well as off the coasts of Japan and the United States.

TROPICAL STORMS

Waterspouts occur in tropical regions such as the Caribbean Sea off Jamaica (above). Many do not last long and may not be reported if no ships are in the area.

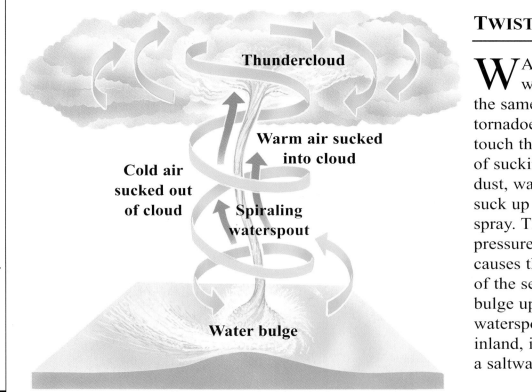

Thundercloud

Warm air sucked into cloud

Cold air sucked out of cloud

Spiraling waterspout

Water bulge

TWISTING AIR

WATERSPOUTS work in much the same way as tornadoes. When they touch the sea, instead of sucking up dirt and dust, waterspouts suck up water and spray. The low air pressure in the funnel causes the surface of the sea or lake to bulge upward. If the waterspout moves inland, it can cause a saltwater rain storm.

FLORIDA KEYS

This waterspout (above) was seen in the Florida Keys. There are over 400 waterspouts a year around this island chain off the southeastern USA. Although waterspouts extend downward from thunderclouds, they sometimes occur in good weather from small clouds. Most waterspouts are from 20 to 200 feet (6 to 60 meters) in diameter. Sometimes they even appear in pairs.

BOAT DAMAGE

ALL violent storms cause damage, as the photograph below shows. Waterspouts are not as violent as some other spinning storms, but people in boats have to be careful to keep away from them while they are sailing in open water.

STORM FORECAST

METEOROLOGISTS study weather reports from many sources. The reports give them an early warning when violent storms are developing. Then they can report the danger in their weather forecasts. There are more than 3,500 weather observation stations around the world, where temperature, air pressure, and wind speed are constantly being measured.

Satellites, planes, and weather balloons are used to observe and measure conditions higher up in the atmosphere.

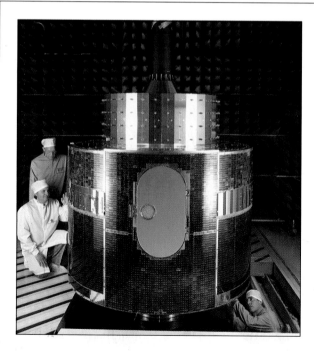

METEOSAT

SCIENTISTS (left) check a weather satellite before a rocket takes it into space. The satellite beams picture signals to weather stations on earth. These pictures are checked by meteorologists to see if hurricanes are developing.

IN ORBIT

Above is an artist's impression of a weather satellite orbiting the earth. Four satellites in the right positions can photograph the whole earth. They stay in position by orbiting at exactly the same speed as the earth's rotation.

INFRARED

The satellite picture above shows a hurricane in different shades of red. It was taken using an infrared camera, which measures heat rather than light waves.

WEATHER AIRPLANE

THIS weather plane has a long probe in its nose that measures air conditions at different levels of the atmosphere. The plane is also fitted with special radar equipment that gives a clear picture of all the cloud patterns.

TAKING PRECAUTIONS

A HURRICANE'S path can often be accurately forecast so that people can take precautions and, perhaps, leave the area. Tornadoes are more sudden and difficult to predict. Some houses in high-risk areas have an underground storm cellar. If people are outside and see a tornado, they should move quickly away from the tornado's path and, if possible, warn others. If there is no time to escape, it is best to lie flat in the nearest ditch.

FOLLOW THE SIGNS
If a hurricane warning is given, people in parts of the USA can follow signs to leave the area. The one above is in southern Louisiana, near the Gulf of Mexico.

STILT HOUSES

IN many parts of the world, houses are built on stilts to protect them from floods caused by tropical storms. These houses (left) are in Kota Kinabalu, capital of the Malaysian state of Sabah, on the island of Borneo. The city is on the coast of the South China Sea, and is always at risk from typhoons.

HURRICANE DAM

THE Fox Point hurricane barrier dam (right) was built on the Providence River, in Rhode Island, USA, in 1966. It is closed during hurricanes to protect Providence, the state capital, from flooding. In 1938, 258 people in the city were killed by floods.

FLOOD BARRIER

It is difficult to protect Bangladesh from flooding because it is in such a low-lying area. High barriers, such as the one below, have to be built. Even with these barriers, two-thirds of the country is flooded for part of the year. Most of the barriers have to be built by hand.

BIGGEST STORMS

ISASTROUS STORMS happen often in the world. The region north of the Bay of Bengal has had terrible storms for centuries. In 1737, a cyclone hit the coast and about 300,000 people were drowned.

Other large storms include a typhoon that hit Indonesia in 1881, killing 300,000 people. In 1900, a hurricane killed about 6,000 people in Texas, USA. In 1974, Hurricane Fifi hit Honduras, in Central America, leaving about 8,000 people dead.

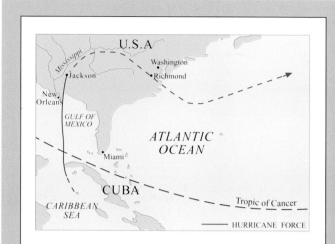

HURRICANE CAMILLE

IN 1969, Hurricane Camille killed over 250 people in the USA. The map above shows its nine-day track. It caused a storm surge of 25 feet (7.6 meters) on the Mississippi coast.

HURRICANE ANDREW

In 1992, the huge Hurricane Andrew (left) passed over the Bahamas and Florida, and headed for Louisiana and the Gulf of Mexico. There was plenty of advance warning, and millions of people were evacuated, but 54 were killed. Damage (right) cost billions of dollars.

CYCLONE FLOODS

BANGLADESH (below) has had many flood disasters. Some experts say that, in 1970, a million people were killed after a cyclone. The world's worst tornado disaster also happened in Bangladesh in 1989. The town of Shaturia was destroyed, with the loss of 1300 lives.

GLOBAL CLIMATE

HURRICANES and tornadoes are part of the whole earth's climate. When the sun's heat reaches the earth's surface, it warms the air. Warm air is light and rises, but cold air is heavier and sinks. This movement of air creates wind. Winds can cause storms and the problems that often follow. Some scientists think that the earth's climate is slowly changing. These changes might cause more extreme storms.

STIRRING UP THE OCEANS

STORMY skies probably pleased the fishermen in a boat off the Malaysian coast (above). There will be more fish to catch because storms stir up food for the fish.

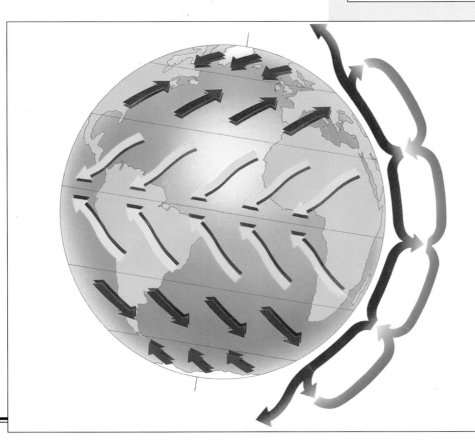

THE WORLD'S WINDS

THERE is a pattern to the world's winds. As warm air rises at the equator, it is replaced by cooler air from the poles. Wind direction is affected by the earth's rotation. In tropical regions, where hurricanes form, winds blow from east to west. These are called the trade winds.

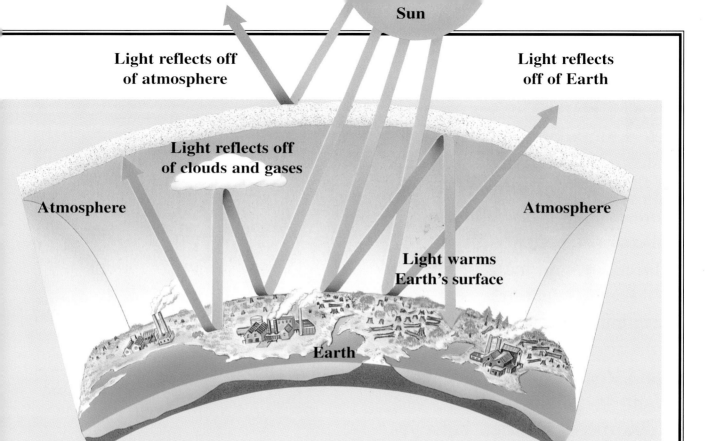

Sun

Light reflects off of atmosphere

Light reflects off of Earth

Light reflects off of clouds and gases

Atmosphere

Atmosphere

Light warms Earth's surface

Earth

GREENHOUSE EFFECT

Some scientists think that the earth and its oceans are warming up. This change might cause more extreme winds. The warming is partly caused by so-called "greenhouse gases" in the atmosphere, which come mainly from the fuels people burn. The gases increase the "greenhouse effect" by trapping heat and stopping it from going back into space.

FORCE	NAME	KPH	MPH	EFFECTS
8	Gale	62-74	39-46	**Twigs broken off trees**
9	Strong gale	75-88	47-54	**Slight damage to buildings**
10	Storm	89-102	55-63	**Trees uprooted**
11	Violent storm	103-118	64-73	**Widespread damage**
12	Hurricane	119 and above	74 and above	**Violent destruction**

BEAUFORT SCALE

THE Beaufort number scale is used to describe different wind speeds. Numbers zero to seven describe winds from "calm" to "moderate gale." Hurricanes, the strongest winds, are number twelve, the top of the scale.

TODAY AND TOMORROW

ALTHOUGH we cannot stop nature's extreme storms, we can improve our knowledge of them. If we understand hurricanes and tornadoes better, we can forecast them more accurately. In some parts of the world, computers help create better warning systems. More shelters and storm cellars are being built in danger zones.

In many countries, however, people do not have the resources to cope with natural disasters and will continue to need help from the rest of the world.

AIR POLLUTION

The greenhouse gases that cause global warming come from air pollution. These gases are caused mainly by the burning of coal, oil, and gas. Factories, such as

DANGER ZONE

WHEN houses are built near shorelines in danger zones, few can withstand hurricane winds and storm surges. In 1992, many homes (left) on the Florida coast were destroyed by Hurricane Andrew.

the mining complex in Australia shown above, are some of the greatest sources of waste gases. The countries of the world need to agree to reduce air pollution and the greenhouse effect.

TELEVISION NEWS

SOME television channels are devoted to forecasting the weather. In danger zones especially, such channels can save lives. If there is enough warning, people can leave the risk area in time and without panic.

STUDYING WEATHER

Information from weather stations, such as this one (right) on a farm in Bolivia, can help meteorologists make sense of weather data from large centers and satellites. They can also forecast local storms. Each day, we learn better ways of forecasting.

GLOSSARY

Atmosphere The layer of air surrounding Earth

Climate The overall weather conditions of an area

Clockwise Describing something turning in a circle that moves in the same direction as a clock's hands

Counter-clockwise Describing something turning in a circle that moves in the opposite direction as a clock's hands

Cyclone A tropical storm, or hurricane, especially in the Indian Ocean

Dam A barrier built across a river to control the flow of its water

Delta A fan-shaped area of low-lying land at the mouth of some rivers where the river splits into many smaller channels

Equator An imaginary circle that stretches around the middle of the earth

Evacuate To escape from a danger area

Eye A calm area in the center of a hurricane

Front An area where a mass of warm air meets a mass of cold air

Global warming An increase in the earth's temperatures caused by pollution

Greenhouse effect The trapping of the sun's warmth inside the earth's atmosphere

Greenhouse gas Any of the gases, such as carbon dioxide, that cause the greenhouse effect

Hemisphere A half of the earth. The northern hemisphere is above the equator; the southern hemisphere is below the equator.

Meteorologist A scientist who studies the weather

Monsoon A seasonal wind that brings heavy rains

Orbit	To travel around an object, such as a star or planet
Plankton	Tiny plants and animals that drift near the surface of the ocean
Pole	The northernmost or southernmost point of Earth. The North Pole is in the Arctic region and the South Pole is in Antarctica.
Pollution	Harmful substances that damage the air, water, or soil
Probe	A device for measuring and testing
Radar	A radio detection system for detecting the position and movement of things, such as clouds or airplanes
Satellite	A device that orbits Earth and sends back information
Storm surge	A sudden rise in sea level caused by a storm, producing floods
Thundercloud	A big, dark cloud that brings thunder, lightning, and heavy rain
Trade wind	A major wind that blows westward near the equator
Tropics	The hottest part of Earth, between two imaginary lines, called the tropic of Cancer and the tropic of Capricorn, that stretch around the world north and south of the equator.
Twister	Another word for a tornado
Typhoon	A tropical storm, or hurricane, in the western Pacific Ocean
Waterspout	A tornado that forms over water
Weather balloon	A balloon that is sent high into the atmosphere to gather information on the weather
Whirlwind	A column of air that spins around and around
Willy-willy	An Australian term for a cyclone, or hurricane

INDEX

4 5 6 7 8 9 0 Printed in the U.S.A. 7 6 5 4 3 2 1